The GIFT *of* RECONCILIATION

Family Guide

AUTHORS

Rev. Richard N. Fragomeni

Jean Marie Hiesberger

Silver Burdett Ginn Religion
A Scott Foresman Imprint
GLENVIEW, IL

Art Credits

Cover Border: Nancy Tobin

Illustrators: Winky Adam: 13b; 21b. David Klug: 15. Anni Matsick: 9b; 12m; 14; 18. Phil Wilson: 16.

Logos/borders: Nancy Tobin

Photo Credits

Cover: Silver Burdett Ginn

All photographs are by Silver Burdett Ginn (SBG) unless otherwise noted.

6: t. Melanie Carr/Viesti Collection. 8: b. Robert Brenner/PhotoEdit. 9: t. Myrleen Ferguson/PhotoEdit. 12: t. Tony Freman/PhotoEdit; b. Jan Cobb/The Image Bank. 17: Myrleen Ferguson/PhotoEdit. 20: Richard Hutchings/PhotoEdit. 21: Myrleen Ferguson/PhotoEdit. 23: Barrie Fanton/Omni Photo Communications, Inc. 26: Superstock.

Acknowledgments

Contributing Writer: Alison J. Berger
Advisor: Joyce Solimini

Nihil Obstat
Kathleen Flanagan, S.C., Ph.D., *Censor Librorum*

Imprimatur
✠Most Reverend Frank J. Rodimer
Bishop of Paterson
October 26, 1998

The *nihil obstat* and *imprimatur* are official declarations that a book or pamphlet is free of doctrinal and moral error. No implication is contained therein that those who have granted the *nihil obstat* and *imprimatur* agree with the contents, opinions, or statements expressed.

Acknowledgments

All adaptations of Scripture are based on *The New American Bible with Revised New Testament*, copyright ©1986 by the Confraternity of Christian Doctrine, Washington, D.C.

Excerpts from the English translation of the *Rite of Penance* © 1974, International Committee on English in the Liturgy, Inc. All rights reserved.

1 2 3 4 5 6 7 8 9 10 - GB - 08 07 06 05 04 03 02 01 00 99

Contents

Reconciliation and the Gift of Family

As the parent of a child who is preparing to celebrate Reconciliation for the first time, you are invited to experience with your child the gifts of joy, peace, forgiveness, and new life that God offers through Jesus Christ in this sacrament. This can be a meaningful and exciting time for the entire family.

Whether you are preparing your child at home or supporting the preparation that takes place in a classroom setting, this Family Guide is for you! In addition to five three-part lessons, this guide includes articles written just for parents. You will also find ideas for family prayer and activities. Making these next few weeks a special time in the life of your family is a great way to thank God for the gift that your child is to you. It can also help your child experience your family as a special gift from God.

As a parent, you are your child's primary religious educator. Your child watches what you do, absorbs your values, and looks to you for guidance.

It is through you that your child learns to relate to God and others.

It is through you that your child learns to relate to God and others. Modeling for your child an openness to receiving the gift of God's unconditional love is perhaps the core of your parental responsibility as primary religious educator.

In all of this, the good news is that you are not alone. This Family Guide is one of many resources available to you. Your parish staff and your child's religion teacher or catechist can offer additional support and assistance. Most importantly you can trust that the Holy Spirit will guide your efforts as you help prepare your child to celebrate the sacrament, and the gift, of Reconciliation.

Getting Started . . .

The following prayers can help you get started on the journey to celebrating Reconciliation with your child. The first prayer is just for you. The second prayer is to share with your family. For both prayers, you might consider praying just a few lines at a time throughout your child's preparation.

A Parent's Prayer

Lord, help me always to seek you above all,
and to see your face in the faces of children everywhere.
Help me to reflect your love to them
in all that I do and say.
Make me an instrument of your peace, Lord,
a reconciling person who chooses peace for myself
and encourages peace among others.
When I fall short of being the person
you call me to be,
give me the faith and the humility to turn to you,
so that my child might also
seek the embrace of your love.
Give me a merciful heart that is patient
and forgiving so that my child, your child,
may believe in and accept
the gift of your unconditional love
and enjoy the new life that you offer us in Jesus Christ
through the power of the Holy Spirit. Amen.

A Family Prayer

Make us ready, Lord, to celebrate your gift of forgiveness. Make our hearts clean. Keep us faithful in thought, word, and deed. Stay close to us always as we live in your Holy Spirit. Heal us, Lord, so we can remember with joy the new life you gave us in the gift of Jesus. Hold us close to you, Jesus, so that we may always be ready to follow your ways. Amen.

Introducing Your

As you guide your child's preparation for his or her first celebration of Reconciliation, we trust that the THE GIFT OF RECONCILIATION student text will serve as a valuable tool for discovering, learning, and celebrating together as a family.

Family Time

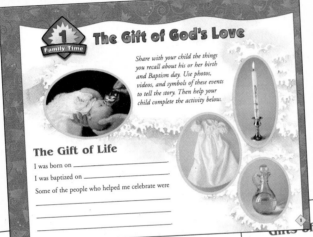

Learning Time

Prayer Time

Child's Book

 Family Time

Each lesson begins with an opportunity for families to share their experiences related to the theme. This family sharing prior to Learning Time prepares children to understand what they are about to learn in the context of their own family experiences.

 Learning Time

Each lesson unfolds in a tried-and-true three-step process that builds on the child's experience, presents Scripture and Tradition in an interesting and meaningful way, and leads your child to pray and to celebrate with the faith community.

1 Discovering God in Our Lives
Through stories and activities, your child is invited to discover God in everyday experiences that are related to the theme of each lesson.

2 Meeting God in the Word and Tradition
At the core of each lesson is an illustrated Scripture story followed by a presentation of Catholic Tradition that supports your child's sacramental preparation.

3 Living with God in Our Lives
As Learning Time concludes, your child is encouraged to integrate into his or her life what he or she has learned.

Prayer Time

You are invited to share in a special prayer celebration at the end of each lesson. Each celebration is flexible and simple enough to use at home. Or you may be invited to celebrate with other families whose children are preparing for the sacrament of Reconciliation.

1 The Gift of God's Love

REFLECTING God's Love

It may seem incredible, but your child's image of God is very closely related to his or her image of YOU! If you are loving and affectionate, your child can readily believe in a loving and caring God. A child who is unfamiliar with love and affection may find it more difficult to believe in such a God. The same goes for forgiveness. If your child sees that you find it difficult to forgive with no strings attached, he or she may find it difficult to believe that God forgives in this way. The next time you look in the mirror, remember that in your child's eyes, your face may be the face of God!

Food for thought: In your life, who has "mirrored" God for you?

THE "IOU" CHALLENGE

So often when someone does us a favor, we immediately want to return the favor. The favors that God does, however, can never be adequately returned; nor does God even want us to try. Our response of gratitude is enough for God.

To help your family appreciate that sometimes a response of gratitude is enough, do a special favor for each person in your family this week. Give your family an opportunity to experience your love as a gift, pure and simple. If they try to do something in return, remind them that God does not keep score and neither will you!

WHAT DO I KNOW ABOUT PRAYER?

It has long been said that the best way to learn to pray is to pray. Sometimes we spend too much time trying to figure out the best way to pray, the proper way to do it, and when or where to do it. As a parent, you may want your child to be more comfortable with prayer or more committed to it than you are. Whatever you (or your children!) decide about your family's prayer life, keep in mind that it's more important *that* you pray than *how, when,* or *where* you pray.

Activity

IT'S YOUR CHOICE . . .

❀ Make a list of questions you and your child have about the sacrament of Reconciliation. Look for answers in the student text (including the Glossary) or ask other parents or catechists.

❀ As a family, take a nature walk. Search for special gifts of creation you can give thanks for.

❀ Look up information about the patron saint of each family member (the saints whose names you received at Baptism). Check out your public library or the parish or school library for resources.

❀ Make a scrapbook of your child's Baptism. Include the baptismal certificate, photos, captions, and symbols—such as those of water, light, and life.

Reviewing Lesson 1

In this lesson we help the children recognize the gift of God's love in creation, in the sacraments, and in people who reflect God's love.

"What Do I Need?"

- student text
- pencils or pens
- crayons or markers
- Baptism memorabilia
- a family Bible
- a bowl of water

Emphasize that your child is a special gift from God.

 ## Family Time

The first page of every lesson includes an activity for your family to complete at home with the child preparing for First Reconciliation. "The Gift of Life" on page 1 of the student text invites you to recall memories of your child's birth and Baptism. As you help your child fill in the information about these special events, be sure to include godparents and people who may have traveled from a distance to celebrate with your family. Emphasize to your child that he or she is a special gift from God in your life, in the lives of your family and friends, and in the life of the Church. Share with your child the joy and pride you felt at his or her Baptism.

Learning Time

1 Discovering God in Our Lives

In this part of the lesson, your child begins to explore his or her own life experience in connection to the lesson. On pages 2 and 3, your child learns about different kinds of gifts. Explain that giving gifts is one way that people show love for one another. Help your child identify some of the gifts that God gives, such as the rainbow and the butterfly. Ask your child what other gifts from God he or she discovered and drew a picture of on page 3.

2 Meeting God in the Word and Tradition

The Scripture story on pages 4 and 5 tells about two important events in Jesus' life: his presentation and his baptism. While the dedication of the infant Jesus in the Temple does not carry exactly the same meaning as infant Baptism today, both celebrate the gift of God's love and the parents' response to that love. In Baptism, God forgives sins and calls us to live our faith in the community of the Church.

On pages 6 and 7, the children read about God's love in the sacraments of initiation (Baptism, Confirmation, Eucharist) and in the sacrament of Reconciliation. The Scripture verse in the activity on page 7 summarizes the good news that through Jesus, we are reconciled with God and have eternal life.

Encourage your child to say a prayer of thanks with you each day for a week.

3 Living with God in Our Lives

The material on pages 8 and 9 helps your child identify several different ways we experience and respond to God's love. Encourage your child to say a prayer of thanks with you each day for a week. Suggest using the verses from Psalm 36 on page 8 and the poetic prayer "We Give Thanks" on page 9. Practice with your child the sign-language gestures for "Thank you, God." Plan a time when you will complete the Family Time activity on page 9, which will help your child review the We Believe statements.

Thank you,   *God.*

✹ Prayer Time

The prayer celebration on page 10 gives you an opportunity to recall your child's Baptism. The student text suggests one way to do this. You may want to choose your own special Scripture passage, gesture, or response. Giving everyone in your family a chance to "come to the water" can help renew your faith and your commitment to God and one another.

2 The Gift of Jesus

Following the Spirit

What do you think it means to follow the Spirit? Is it a matter of listening more closely to the still, small voice of God? Does it mean taking more time to pray? Or doing what Jesus would do? As you discover what it means for *you* to follow the Spirit, keep in mind that being a *disciple*, a follower of Jesus, involves *discipline*. Consider exploring some spiritual disciplines for a week. Set aside time each day for prayer or Scripture study. At the end of the week, mark your calendar for two more weeks. Remember that it takes about three weeks to develop a habit!

The Miracle of Life

There is no greater miracle than life itself, especially new life. Each time a child is conceived and born, parents are sharing with God the awesome privilege of creating a brand-new life. In raising a child, parents share intimately in the experience of cultivating and helping this new life to grow.

Take a few minutes this week to reflect on the miracle of new life.

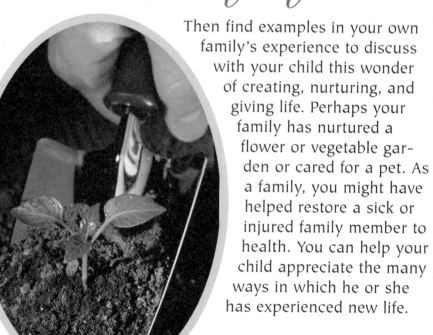

Then find examples in your own family's experience to discuss with your child this wonder of creating, nurturing, and giving life. Perhaps your family has nurtured a flower or vegetable garden or cared for a pet. As a family, you might have helped restore a sick or injured family member to health. You can help your child appreciate the many ways in which he or she has experienced new life.

Getting Focused in Prayer

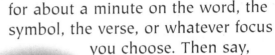

Just as some people need eyeglasses to improve their vision, many of us need something to improve or focus our attention in prayer. It helps to focus on a word or a phrase, a religious picture or symbol, a Scripture verse or a story. First, invite everyone to focus quietly

for about a minute on the word, the symbol, the verse, or whatever focus you choose. Then say, "Lord, we thank you for this gift of . . ." followed by the chosen focus. Invite each person to add a sentence or two. Conclude with "Lord, we thank you for this gift of . . ." once again.

Activity

BE A GIFT TO SOMEONE

As a family, decide this week on one way that you can reach out to someone in need. When we take the time to do something special for someone without expecting anything in return, what we do is truly a gift.

Here are some things you can do as a family. Make sure each person shares in the giving opportunity. Your children probably have some great ideas, too!

🎁 Bake a cake or prepare a meal for someone who needs some cheering up or encouragement.

🎁 Help prepare or serve a meal in a community soup kitchen or shelter for homeless people.

🎁 Make your own greeting cards and bring them to residents in a nursing home or another health-care facility.

🎁 Donate clothes and toys to an organization that will distribute them to people who can use them.

Reviewing Lesson 2

In this lesson we help the children appreciate that they are all called to a life of holiness as they follow Jesus, live in the Spirit, and participate in the sacraments of the Church.

"What Do I Need?"
- student text
- pencils or pens
- a family Bible
- a potted flower seed

Some people bring out the best in us.

 **Family Time**

In the activity on page 11, you can help your child discover some of the things that make a person special. These might include having a sense of humor, taking time to listen, sharing similar interests, or simply being a friend. As you share with your child what you believe is special about Jesus, you might share a favorite story about Jesus or a story that Jesus told that has special meaning for you. Help your child appreciate that Jesus is a special gift from God. This might be a good time to use the prayer suggestion on page 13 of this guide, using the word *Jesus* to help your family get focused for a brief time of prayer.

 Learning Time

1 Discovering God in Our Lives

"A Special Guest" on pages 12 and 13 might remind your child of a time when your own family has prepared for a visit from someone special. In reviewing this story and the activity that follows, help your child appreciate that some people bring out the best in us. Help your child identify specific people whose opinions really matter and who encourage your child to be on his or her best behavior. Share some examples from your own life.

2 Meeting God in the Word and Tradition

Use the illustrations on pages 14 and 15 to help your child review the Scripture story. The first scene shows Jesus at the Last Supper, promising to send the Holy Spirit to his disciples. The second scene shows flames of fire above the disciples' heads. Artists have traditionally used this image to show the Holy Spirit descending upon Jesus' followers at Pentecost. The third scene shows Saint Peter talking to the people. Use the Glossary in the student text to review the words *disciples*, *repent*, *Church*, *sin*, *forgiveness*, *Pentecost*, and *healing*.

Pages 16 and 17 describe how the Holy Spirit helps the Church community live and grow in the ways that God wants us to. Ask your child to tell you what makes *holiness* and *sin* opposites. (Holiness brings us closer to God and one another; sin separates us from God and one another.) Give your child an opportunity to use the prayer he or she wrote to lead your family in prayer at an evening meal this week.

3 Living with God in Our Lives

The activity on page 18 asks your child to identify some of the things a Catholic might think, say, or do. Page 19 presents an opportunity for your family to give thanks for the gift of new life and to talk about special relationships. Review the We Believe statements with your child by reading them aloud and leaving out key words for your child to fill in.

Prayer Time

The prayer celebration on page 20 invites you to share the parable of the Sower and the Seed to help your child appreciate that the seed of faith that Jesus has planted within each of us needs some help to grow. You may wish to read Psalm 65 from a Bible, inviting your family to say the response after every two or three verses.

HOLINESS

SIN

Holiness brings us closer to God and one another; sin separates us from God and one another.

3 Responding to the Gift

GOD, OUR CENTER

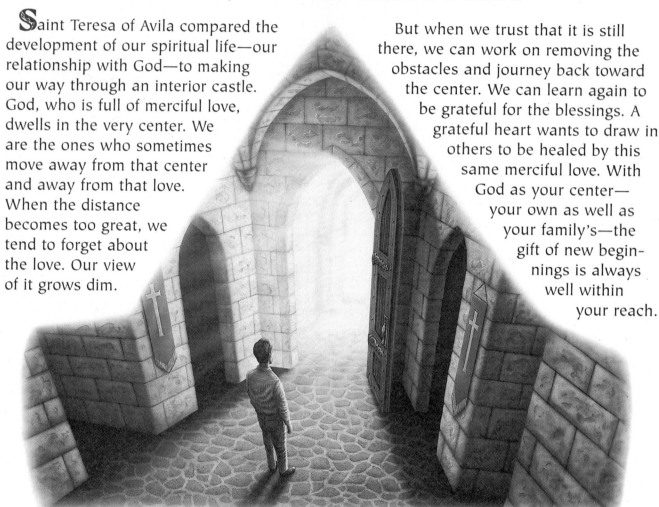

Saint Teresa of Avila compared the development of our spiritual life—our relationship with God—to making our way through an interior castle. God, who is full of merciful love, dwells in the very center. We are the ones who sometimes move away from that center and away from that love. When the distance becomes too great, we tend to forget about the love. Our view of it grows dim.

But when we trust that it is still there, we can work on removing the obstacles and journey back toward the center. We can learn again to be grateful for the blessings. A grateful heart wants to draw in others to be healed by this same merciful love. With God as your center—your own as well as your family's—the gift of new beginnings is always well within your reach.

Cultivating GRATITUDE

When we sin, we make a conscious choice to turn away from God, Jesus, and one another. Through Reconciliation, we experience a conversion, a turning back to God and the Church. Conversion is a lifelong process in which the Holy Spirit works through us, transforming our lives to the image of Christ.

A prudent and sincere examination of conscience can be an instrument of God's grace and blessing for you and your family. It can be a time of affirmation as well as challenge. It can help make us aware of our strengths and our goodness as well as our weaknesses. It moves us toward a response of gratitude for God's gifts of love and mercy.

A Mealtime Prayer

Father, we thank you for the gift of this meal we are about to share. And we thank you for one another. Fill our hearts with gratitude and praise each day as we learn to treasure your gifts of love and mercy, especially as we experience that love within our family. Amen.

Activity

AN AWARENESS EXERCISE

Use these questions to help you and your family awaken to the abundant blessings that God offers you each and every day.

✔ Do we set aside time each day to talk to God? to listen to God? to see the love of God in one another?

✔ What are some of the ways we are reminded of God's presence in our home and in our lives each day?

✔ When something good happens, do we give thanks to God? In times of trouble, do we trust in God's love?

✔ Could we share with one another or keep a family journal of the blessings we are grateful for each day?

Family Blessings Book

January–June

Reviewing Lesson 3

In this lesson we invite the children to say Yes! to God's gifts of love and mercy by gratefully sharing these gifts with others.

"What Do I Need?"

- student text
- pencils or pens
- crayons or colored pencils
- hearts made from construction paper

Help your child develop an attitude of gratitude.

Family Time

The activity on page 21 helps your child explore ways he or she has expressed thanks to others. This lesson presents an excellent opportunity for you to help your child develop an attitude of gratitude and to appreciate the importance of this virtue to Jesus. Consider sharing the story of the ten lepers from Luke 17:11–19 or a psalm of thanksgiving such as Psalm 118. Pages 57 and 58 of the student text also include some prayers of praise and thanksgiving that your family might share together.

Learning Time

1 Discovering God in Our Lives

The story on pages 22 and 23 is about an offer of friendship that is rejected at first and then extended again. Use the "Talk About It" questions on page 23 to review the story with your child. You might then explore with your child what might have happened if Debra had given up on Elana. With your child, imagine some of the great times that Elana and Debra shared once they became friends. Help your child appreciate how forgiveness and second chances can lead to reconciliation and new beginnings, such as new or renewed friendships.

2 Meeting God in the Word and Tradition

Use the illustrations on pages 24 and 25 to help your child further explore this familiar parable of the Prodigal Son. In this retelling the story is less about the son's repentance than about the father's gift of merciful love. A powerful story to assure your child of God's unconditional love, it can also help lay the foundation for your child's understanding of an examination of conscience as he or she takes a closer look at the choices that the son makes along the way. Pages 26 and 27 help your child consider his or her own unloving choices. Use the Glossary in the student text to teach or review the meaning of the terms *mercy* and *examination of conscience*.

3 Living with God in Our Lives

Invite your child to share his or her responses to the questions on page 28. Then talk about similar situations that may have taken place in your own family. Find creative ways to pray the prayer on page 29. Prayerful gestures can be powerful instruments of growth in your family's prayer life. The Family Time suggestion invites you to encourage one another in this. Also consider using the We Believe statements as a springboard for a prayer of gratitude at a family meal this week. For example, "Thank you, Holy Spirit, for helping us respond to God's love."

Prayerful gestures can be powerful instruments of growth in your family's prayer life.

✸ Prayer Time

Consider using the prayer celebration on page 30 at home this week. Encourage your entire family to actively respond to God's gifts by sharing these gifts with one another or with friends or neighbors. Invite each person to write on his or her construction-paper heart a simple promise to share God's love, mercy, or forgiveness with someone. Then place the hearts where everyone will be reminded of his or her promise.

I forgive you for breaking my toy.

I will help you set the table.

I will read you a story.

4 The Gift of Forgiveness

The Call to Forgive

In the Lord's Prayer we say, "Forgive us our trespasses as we forgive those who trespass against us." If you've ever found it difficult to forgive someone, this can present quite a challenge. Or perhaps you find comfort in knowing that God will forgive you as generously as you've forgiven others. A closer look at just how tremendously and mercifully God forgives and loves would remind you that God's gifts are not measured or limited by how much you have forgiven or loved others. Still, as a Christian, you are called to forgive and love others. And God often forgives and loves through you! How are you answering the call to forgive others in your life? What motivates your offers of forgiveness?

KEEPING THE PEACE

Some of us are natural peacemakers: people who are great at helping to resolve difficulties between other people, people who are often called upon to "smooth things over" or "calm the waters." Are you one of those people?

On a daily basis, keeping the peace often has more to do with dealing with the innocent or not-so-innocent mistakes that people make, sometimes at our expense. Our patience can be easily tried. As sacramental people called to be signs of God's love and mercy, we are called to offer forgiveness at all times, with or without words.

A PRAYER FOR "LETTING GO"

*I*n the spirit of the new millennium, gather your family together for a time of prayer in which you "let go" of grudges or any "debts" you think someone owes you. If you're the one holding the grudge, or feeling as if someone owes you big time, you might ask the other person for forgiveness. Then you might offer that same person your forgiveness. This can be a good way to wipe the slate clean and begin to rebuild any relationships in the family that may be suffering, even if only slightly, due to the sin in our lives. Pray that God will help you to forgive one another completely. And vow never to bring up a matter again once you have "let go" of it in prayer.

A LEARNING GAME

Materials: Ten or more 5"x 8" index cards with descriptions of familiar actions that could take place in the family. Half of the cards will have sins written on them. The other half will have mistakes written on them.

Directions: Print a descriptive statement of a sin or a mistake on each card. Also print the letter **S** or the letter **M** below each statement to identify it as a sin or a mistake. Shuffle the cards. Then take turns drawing cards. The person who draws the top card reads the statement to the player on his or her left. The player on the left decides if the statement describes a sin or a mistake. The player on the left draws the next card, and the play continues until all cards have been drawn.

I stole candy from the store.

I left my bike out in the rain.

Reviewing Lesson 4

In this lesson we help the children appreciate the joy of both receiving and offering the gift of forgiveness as they take the first steps toward reconciliation.

"What Do I Need?"

- student text
- pencils or pens
- colored pencils or markers
- a gift or a card for your child that expresses forgiveness

Sometimes reconciliation does not happen until much later. Forgiveness is the first step.

 ## Family Time

As you complete the activity on page 31 with your child, take time to find examples that can help both you and your child answer each question clearly and honestly. Try to focus on simple experiences of forgiveness within the family—between siblings, between parents, or between parent and child. Encourage your child to identify how things felt before and after the moment of forgiveness or reconciliation. Note that sometimes reconciliation does not happen until much later. Forgiveness is the first step.

 ## Learning Time

1 Discovering God in Our Lives

In reviewing the story that begins on page 32, ask your child to tell you in order the four story parts in the activity on page 33. Help your child understand what Andy's mother means when she talks about taking the first step. Try to think of additional examples to share. Then ask your child when he or she thinks Andy's mother began to change from being angry to being sorry and how that must have felt to her.

2 Meeting God in the Word and Tradition

The story of the Good Shepherd on pages 34 and 35 often inspires in children a genuine hope and trust in a very caring God. Read this story with your child. Point out details in the illustrations such as the winding paths, the rocky terrain, and the changing expressions on the shepherd's face. Consider sharing additional books, pictures, and information or objects that can help your child further appreciate how much a shepherd cares for his sheep.

In reviewing the text on pages 36 and 37, use the Glossary in the student text to review the definitions of the words *sin* and *reconciliation*. The exercise on page 37 can help your child distinguish mistakes from sins.

3 Living with God in Our Lives

On page 38 your child learns that both Eucharist and Reconciliation reconcile us with God and one another. Help your child appreciate that Penance is a positive means of growth and maturity that leads to more peaceful living. When we are free from the guilt or burden of sin, God's love can grow within us more fully. Reaffirm these points by reviewing the We Believe statements together. Consider praying the "Prayer to Be Joyful" each day with your child. Use the Family Time prayer as appropriate.

Prayer Time

This simple ritual celebrates the joy of reconciliation. It also presents an opportunity to teach or review an act of contrition. Additional prayers of contrition can be found on page 56 in the student text. If you use this ritual at home, present a card or gift that expresses your forgiveness of your child and assure your son or daughter that God forgives in even greater ways. Help your child and your entire family appreciate that God is truly joyful over us, especially when we accept and celebrate the gifts that God offers us.

When we are free from the guilt or burden of sin, God's love can grow within us more fully.

5 Celebrating the Gift

The Ministry of Reconciliation

*I*n helping other people, especially our children, make peace with one another, we might keep in mind the image of clay in a potter's hands. Allowing the forgiving love of Christ to shape and mold us, freeing us to become completely new creations, makes it possible for us to invite others to experience the same. Recalling the joy and the healing of our own new beginnings can make a world of difference in all our peacemaking efforts, among others or between ourselves and someone else.

Our Vocation to Blessedness

*G*od has placed a desire for happiness in each of our hearts. This desire draws us, ultimately, to the only One who can give us complete and perfect happiness. We discover quickly enough that wealth, fame, and power—things that are considered sources of joy in this world—offer only a fragile, empty, temporary sort of happiness.

In Matthew, Chapter 5, we find the very center of Jesus' teachings: the Beatitudes. In a sense, the Beatitudes present a verbal portrait of Jesus: the poor one, the meek, the merciful, the peacemaker. Simply put, our call to follow Jesus is a call to happiness. And the happiness we experience now is only a glimpse of greater things to come in the eternal kingdom of God.

MAKE ME A BLESSING

One evening this week, invite each member of the family to offer this prayer in the presence of the whole family: "Lord, make me a blessing to my family." Then, together, pray for a desire to follow Jesus more closely each day and to live as Jesus taught so that you can enjoy *all* the blessings that God wants to give you, as individuals and as a family.

•LORD, •MAKE•ME•A•BLESSING•TO•MY•FAMILY•

Activity

BIBLE BOOKMARK

Materials: Wide ribbon, stickers, glue, typed or handwritten copy of the Beatitudes

Directions: Write or print a single beatitude on each ribbon. Or write the beatitude on paper and glue it to the ribbon. Decorate each ribbon with stickers and other items to remind you of the joy that God calls you to. Encourage everyone to keep the bookmarks in their Bibles. Consider making bookmarks to give as gifts. In this way, the members of your own family can share the blessings of God with others.

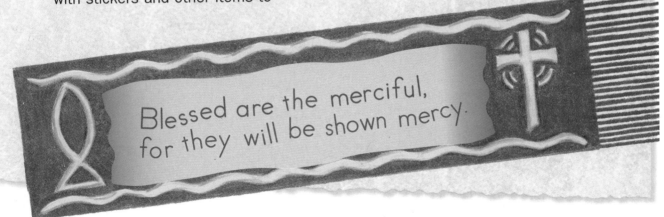

Blessed are the merciful, for they will be shown mercy.

Reviewing Lesson 5

In this lesson we help the children learn the Beatitudes and prepare to celebrate the sacrament of Penance.

"What Do I Need?"

- student text
- pencils or pens
- a family Bible

Explain to your child that Jesus warmly welcomes and embraces all the children who come to him.

Family Time

Begin the Family Time on page 41 by talking about the illustration of Jesus. Explain to your child that Jesus warmly welcomes and embraces all children who come to him. Then share with your child about times when you have experienced the warmth of God's love. The prayer in the student text is the same one found on page 5 of this Family Guide. Pray this with your child. As suggested, be sure to add your own prayers.

Learning Time

1 Discovering God in Our Lives

The story on pages 42 and 43 addresses a question your child may have about celebrating Reconciliation. Do your best to answer his or her questions. Ask your pastor, your child's catechist or teacher, or your sacraments coordinator for help as needed. In reviewing the story, ask if your child thinks Miguel's feelings about the sacrament change by the end of story. Note how Rosa helps Miguel. The two Spanish-language phrases can be translated as "I'll be there in a minute" and "That's OK, little brother."

2 Meeting God in the Word and Tradition

The Scripture story on pages 44 and 45 is Jesus' teaching of the Beatitudes, sometimes called the Sermon on the Mount. The Beatitudes describe how people who love God should try to live each and every day. They also help us anticipate the blessings of living according to Jesus' teachings. As you review pages 46 and 47, help your child anticipate the sacrament as a joyful celebration by recalling the endings of the parables of the Prodigal Son and Lost Sheep. Note that the prayer of blessing on page 47 is from the *Rite of Penance*.

Remind your child that Reconciliation can be celebrated throughout our lives.

3 Living with God in Our Lives

The first paragraph on page 48 reminds us that Reconciliation is not just between God and the individual. Help your child complete the sentences at the bottom of the page. The "Prayer for a Blessing" on page 49 would be appropriate just before the sacramental celebration. Remind your child that this is not meant to be a once-in-a-lifetime opportunity. Reconciliation can be celebrated throughout our lives. Before the Family Time prayer, review the We Believe statements and explore the photograph on pages 48 and 49. Recall together the waters of Baptism. Lead your family to appreciate the feeling of refreshment, enjoyment, and new life that water can give. Note that Reconciliation can be experienced in the same way.

☀ Prayer Time

This prayer ritual emphasizes that the gift of Reconciliation with God and with others is something to celebrate! It will be a time of blessing. Even if your child celebrates this Prayer Time with others in the parish, use it at home as an opportunity to affirm all that your child has learned and experienced in preparing for Reconciliation. Pray together to the Holy Spirit for all the blessings your child hopes to receive in the sacrament of Reconciliation.

5

Models of Forgiveness

In Jesus' own example and in his parables, we find models of forgiveness and compassion. As Christian parents, we are called to do our best to imitate this unconditional love.

The following Scripture passages show us how Jesus demonstrated forgiveness. You may wish to use these passages for personal reflection or share them during family prayer times. Help your children find these Scripture passages by explaining that the books of the Bible are divided into chapters, and each chapter is divided into verses. For example, the parable of the Unforgiving Servant is found in Matthew 18:21–35. The word *Matthew* refers to the Gospel According to Matthew, in the New Testament. The number following the name of the book is the chapter number, Chapter 18. The numbers that follow refer to the verse numbers, verses 21–35.

Jesus' Forgiving Words and Deeds

Matthew 18:21–35	The parable of the Unforgiving Servant
Mark 2:1–12	Jesus forgives and heals a paralyzed man
Mark 2:13–17	Jesus eats with tax collectors and sinners
Luke 7:36–50	Jesus forgives a sorrowful woman
Luke 15:8–10	The parable of the Lost Coin
Luke 18:9–14	The parable of the Pharisee and the Tax Collector
Luke 19:1–10	Jesus forgives Zacchaeus
John 8:1–11	Jesus forgives an adulterous woman

The Sacrament of Reconciliation

Jesus entrusted his mission of healing and forgiveness to the Apostles. He sent them the Holy Spirit to give them the power to forgive sins in his name.

When we choose to act selfishly by putting ourselves ahead of God and others, we sin. A sin is a free decision to do what we know is wrong or to fail to do what we know is right.

Mortal sin is a very serious offense against God and the Christian community. There are three conditions that make a sin mortal: The act must be seriously wrong, we must know that the act is seriously wrong, and we must freely choose to commit the sin. According to Church precepts, Catholic adults are obliged to confess serious sins at least once a year.

A venial sin is a less serious offense. It weakens, but does not destroy, our relationship with God and the Church. Confession of venial sins is strongly recommended.

The Church continues Jesus' mission of forgiveness and healing in the sacrament of Reconciliation. When we confess our sins to the priest, we express our sorrow to God and to the Church. We ask for the grace to resist sin and do better in the future. The priest forgives us and absolves us of our sins in the name of the Father, and of the Son, and of the Holy Spirit. The priest's absolution is also a sign that the Church community forgives us, too. A priest can never reveal what he is told in the sacrament. This is called the seal of confession.

Conflict Resolution Tips
for Families

All families experience conflict. Differences in age, temperament, disposition, interest, and energy levels can kindle flare-ups. Here are a few suggestions for handling family conflicts.

1. **Respond respectfully; don't overreact.**

   Take a deep breath. Count to ten if necessary. Speak calmly. Ask questions without making assumptions or accusations. Remember that you are a role model for your children.

2. **Be impartial.**

   Assess the situation fairly. Make sure any discipline or punishment really fits the crime.

3. **Get to the root of the conflict.**

   Ask (at least in your own mind) what someone's motive might be for doing something selfish or hurtful. For example, did Mary take Lexie's toy just to tease or deliberately to be mean? Might she be trying to get some needed attention?

4. **Evaluate afterward.**

   Once everyone has cooled down a bit, invite the parties involved to share ideas about how the situation could have been handled differently. They could even role-play a different ending. Encourage your children to ask: "What would Jesus do in my place?"

Enhancing Family Spirituality

Here are a few ways to help nurture a living faith for all the members of your family. Begin with the one that is most comfortable. Then challenge yourself to expand your comfort zone!

1. **Pray together.**

   Make room in your family's schedule for some regular prayer time. Session 1 offers some specific suggestions for family prayer.

2. **Discuss religious matters.**

   Talk about local, national, and world events. Discuss the moral message of a movie or TV show. Ask your children what they learned in religion class.

3. **Reflect on God's word.**

   Read aloud one of the Sunday Scripture readings. Pause for a moment of reflection. Then invite all family members to share their thoughts. End with a brief prayer.

4. **Celebrate together.**

   Whenever possible, celebrate the sacraments together. When one child is celebrating the sacrament of Reconciliation for the first time, invite the rest of the family to share in the preparation and celebration.

5. **Serve others together.**

   As a family, do something that will make a difference in another person's or family's life. For example, do chores for an elderly or disabled neighbor. Donate family funds to charity. Take part in an event that benefits unborn children or people who are hungry, homeless, or unemployed.

Embracing
the Gift of Reconciliation

Consider using this simple prayer ritual with your family on a regular basis. It can help nourish the spirit of reconciliation among yourselves and with others.

◆ Turn off the phone, the computer, and the TV. Gather in a comfortable space. Light a candle to remind those gathered that Christ, our Light, is with your family.

◆ Begin with the Sign of the Cross and a familiar prayer, such as the Lord's Prayer.

◆ Read a passage from Scripture or another appropriate reading, story, or poem that inspires a spirit of forgiveness and reconciliation. (See page 28 of this Family Guide for Scripture suggestions.)

◆ Discuss any conflicts or differences that may have arisen among your family recently. Talk about how the Scripture passage, prayer, or reading might relate to the situation. Allow every voice to be heard and given equal respect and attention. Work toward healing any tensions or problems in the spirit of family harmony.

◆ End your family prayer time by inviting family members to share spontaneous prayers in their own words. Conclude with a gesture of reconciliation, such as a handshake or a family hug.